I READ I WRITE

أنا أقرأ أنا أكتب

LAURA BOUSHNAK

Laura Boushnak © 2019

All rights reserved. No part of this work may be reproduced, stored in a retrieval system, distributed, or transmitted in any form or by any means, including photocopying, recording, or other electronic or mechanical methods, without the prior written permission of the publisher, except in the case of brief quotations embodied in critical reviews and certain other noncommercial uses permitted by copyright law.

First published in 2019
Rimal Books
Cyprus
www.rimalbooks.com

ISBN: 978-9963-715-19-0

Book design by Boast Design. www.boastdesign.com
Desktop Publishing by Ready, Design, Print!
Text Editor: Rory Mulholland
Arabic Translation: Basma Badran
Photo Editor: Tarek Al-Ghoussein

Printed in Bosnia and Herzegovina
Grafotisak d.o.o.

# Contents

Foreword — 7

Introduction — 8

Egypt: Illiteracy Classes 2009 — 11

Jordan: Dropout Students 2012 — 27

Yemen: Access to Education 2012 — 39

Tunisia: Students' Union 2013 — 59

Saudi Arabia: Women at Work 2016 — 83

Gaza: Blockade 2016 — 115

I'm in awe of all the women who opened their homes and hearts to me so that I could share their stories. This book is for them, and to all the women who took it upon themselves to clear the path for others.

# Foreword by Hanan Al Shaykh

As I gaze at Laura Boushnak's photographs of young women and mothers from several Arab countries, from Egypt, to Tunisia, Jordan, Palestine's Gaza, to the Kingdom of Saudi Arabia and Yemen, I find myself applauding them as they learn to read and write, scratching at the obsolete tradition with their bare nails, and stirring a breath of life into the stagnation in their core.

Laura, through her photographs, wants us to hear, see, smell, and touch these ladies who have cracked through impasses, seizing the slightest of openings to set out towards the horizon of freedom, especially the freedom to choose.

Through her lens, Laura has succeeded in capturing their lives, with each photograph narrating a story. It is a celebration of the women, and of the housewives who held on to the letters and words like a lifeline, after being worlds apart. To keep on track with time, they seek knowledge and specialisation to become actively engaged in society.

Nevertheless, these photographs are a thorn in the beholder's eye. I, for instance, couldn't but gasp at the oppression befalling women, driving them into illiteracy merely because they're female.

Laura thus takes us to that young lady on the shore, donning a blue head scarf, the colour of the ever fluctuating tide, as if it were a record of the ebb and flow of her life.

Then there's the young woman in a tent, playing that oud which many attempted to snatch from her arms, merely because she's female. I see the veiled woman, wearing full makeup as if to say, "I wear the veil as I please."

I almost hear one asserting, "I don't want a guardian, but a friend for a husband", while another challenges the saying, "a husband or the grave", and one more wondering, "will life walk along or against me?"

In the room of one of the girls in Gaza, darkness reigns due to electricity shortages, and she uses her mobile phone for light. It seems to me that Laura relied on the light shining from the hearts of her subjects, the beating of those hearts, rather than artificial lighting, turning her photographs into works of art, some shrouded in fog, others in light and shadow. It's the eyes in the photos that talk to us, as if the photographer captured fleeting expressions of the soul with her lens, just before they escaped.

I have become captive to these images. Through them, I relived the sadness of my mother Kamleh when she related to me what she said to her family as a 12-year-old kid, "I want to go to school, even pigeons go to school". She had noticed how pigeons understood, and responded to their fancier.

Mother remained "ignorant", faking fainting and sickness on airplanes to hide her inability to read or write and her failure to fill out passenger cards.

I grew accustomed to my mother's pleas, "Why don't you write my life story?" She would say, "It might be more beautiful or more magical than whatever you have just had published."

I was deaf until one day she said, "I was never so desperate to read and write as I am now, if for no other reason than to write my story. Let me tell you how it hurts when a piece of wood and a piece of lead defeat me."

When I asked her what she meant, she said, "Isn't a pencil made of wood and lead?"

# Introduction

I could barely contain my excitement as I graduated from high school in 1995. I wanted to leave Kuwait, where I was born to Palestinian refugee parents, and go to university like the rest of my classmates. My father, however, had other plans. He wanted me to enrol in a "secretarial skills" course, and get a job that would supply me with pocket money until a husband came along and took care of me.

"Had you been born a boy, I would have paid for your education." Those were his words, words that many Arab women have heard, and still do, at some point in their lives.

My immediate rejection of the path he chose for me only boosted my resolve to get a university degree, while the frustration his suggestion instilled in me prompted me, years later, to seek out remarkable stories of women in different countries in the Arab world.

I wanted to underline the obstacles these women faced throughout their lives to gain access to education, and stress the role that education played in their lives.

Looking back at the lives of women in my family, I could identify many of the never-ending ordeals which still dominate the turbulent region, from socio-religious constraints and racism, to political instability and armed conflict coupled with continuous foreign interference.

Dawlat, my maternal grandmother, was married when she was 13, her last year of primary schooling. In 1948, with the creation of the state of Israel, she was forced with her family, parents, and siblings, into exile from their home in Haifa, on the northern coast of Palestine. Soon after my grandfather passed away, leaving her to care for three children.

Embarking on a strenuous journey to find refuge, she finally settled in Irbid, in the north of Jordan. She and her family were granted Jordanian nationality, as were many Palestinian refugees who settled in the Kingdom after fleeing their homes in 1948.

There she was, a young widow with three mouths to feed, refugees in an unfamiliar community. She clung to her conservative traditionalist upbringing, and focused on work. The sewing courses she gave at a refugee camp in the West Bank helped her provide for her family, until Israel seized that area in the 1967 war, depriving her of a crucial means of subsistence.

Living in turbulent times, my mother decided that learning a trade was more important than high school and enrolled in beautician courses at a technical school. In 1966, soon after graduating, she moved to Kuwait to live with her uncle while working at a beauty salon to support her mother.

Then she married my father. He was a Palestinian refugee in Lebanon who sought work in Kuwait along with many others during the oil boom in the early 60s. Their marriage meant that she would quit work, as was customary, to make a home for the children to come.

My father, the family breadwinner, did not believe that providing a decent education for myself was a priority for our household's meagre finances. I understood the financial argument, but I was disappointed at his utter lack of interest in or encouragement of me furthering my studies, which I saw as the only way to better my life as a stateless refugee at the time.

It is a fact that mothers in most countries in the region cannot transfer their nationality to their children. Only the father can. Like many in such situations, I had to deal with the consequences of this restriction which granted me access to Lebanese "travel documents", as my father had, rather than my mother's Jordanian nationality.

Foreigners in Kuwait were generally barred from enrolling at the state university, while private college education was not available. Therefore, I took a receptionist job after graduating from high school at a new American school for girls, to pay fees for a social sciences diploma at the Lebanese University, in parallel with a distance-learning course at the New York Institute of Photography.

In 1998, at the age of 22, I left Kuwait for Lebanon, where I later embarked on a career in the male-dominated profession of journalism. Aside from the day-to-day work, the experiences of my youth were still there, pushing me to seek similar stories to my own.

In my early research for this project, in 2009, I learned in a UN report from 2005 that Arab countries collectively had one of the highest rates of female illiteracy in the world. I was astounded!

Along the way I found out about many other constraints, apart from illiteracy, that women in the region face. These include: difficulties or interruptions in access to school and/or higher education, curricula devoid of real learning, low political awareness and activism, scarcity of jobs for highly-educated women, and wars and internal strife.

All these factors, and many more, hinder a large portion of the people in Arab societies - their women - and hamper developmental efforts for the entire region.

I started the project in 2009, prior to the tumultuous events later dubbed the Arab Spring, which took very different turns in the various countries where they occurred.

Tunisia, where the so-called Jasmine Revolution erupted after a street vendor set himself on fire when police confiscated his produce, has emerged with a progressive new constitution, and recently passed a law penalizing gender-based violence. In Syria, however, the initial peaceful protests soon turned into a complex civil war with regional and international interference, with ongoing repercussions for millions in the region and beyond. Between these extremes, several other countries continue to deal with varying degrees of adversity, with education often a prime victim.

In parallel, it turned out to be a transformative journey for me, professionally and personally, one that changed my work, my perspective on things, and what I was looking for.

In the following pages, I attempt to provide a glimpse into the lives of Arab women trying options they are otherwise barred from in the region, in their quest to improve their life, that of their children and their community.

I've included some of my most moving encounters with outstanding young women and seasoned housewives who are brave enough to break with some social norms in order to give more to their families and their communities.

I always sought a collaborative approach with the women I photographed. I wanted them to actively participate in the experience, in a way that can be reflected in the final photograph. Their candid, hand-written words, complementing their images, were the perfect way to illustrate their involvement and to display their achievements.

Their own personal seal.

# EGYPT
Illiteracy Classes 2009

As the taxi made its way through the bustling streets of Cairo, I felt as though I was stepping into the familiar world of the countless movies, songs, and books produced there, which have influenced millions of Arabs, myself included. From the middle of the 19th century, Egypt gradually became the centre of culture for the entire Arab world, a magnet for writers, musicians, producers, actors, painters, poets, dancers, journalists, and craftspeople. Women played a central role in that great cultural movement, which peaked in the 1960s and then went into slow decline.

Decades later, a 2013 Thomson Reuters Foundation survey of gender experts placed Egypt at the bottom of a ranking of 22 Arab states, citing discriminatory laws, a surge in violence and sexual harassment, and increased Islamic conservatism, after the so-called Arab Spring. In another damning report in 2015, the French Development Agency estimated that the lives of 35% of Egyptian women were severely damaged by their illiteracy.

My taxi ride took me to the suburbs of Cairo, where I was to visit the Association for the Development and Enhancement of Women (ADEW), an independent group running a nine-month literacy programme of daily classes for housewives.

Some of the women in the classes I attended noted with great amusement that I resembled Jackie Chan, the action movie star from Hong Kong. This was a great icebreaker that smoothed the way for the month I would spend sharing a little bit of their lives.

I asked the women to use their newly acquired skill to answer the following question: Why did you decide to learn how to read and write?

من انا
نادية سيد مبارك

"Who am I" were the first words Nadia could write.

لإجلال معوض ٥٣ سنة
تركت المدرسة من اربعين سنة
حصل موقف صعب كانت لازم اساعد ابنه في المدرسة واكتب شكوى وما عرفتش مكان المعلقة صعب وبحرج
تعلمت ان اتعلم علشان أقرأ واكتب من غير علم ظلام اذا اشوف كتابة ومش عارفه أقرأ
كأني متى شايفة في الاول زوجي عرض عشان مش علي أخرج بعدلا أن صممت اني اتعلم

"I left school 45 years ago. I was embarrassed when my son asked me to write a complaint letter to his school and I was unable to help. At the beginning my husband wouldn't allow me to take literacy classes because he didn't want me to leave the house. But I insisted because if I see text and I'm not able to read it it's like being blind." Ejlal Muawad, 53.

سناء محمد سيد   ٣١ سنه
نفسى أتعلم علشان العوامعلات
لأنى بتوه

"I wish to learn to read because I get lost on public transport." Sanaa Sayed, 31.

نادية مصطفى ٣٦ سنة
عايزه أتعلم علشان
أفهم الدنيا وحلمي أتعلم

"I want to learn to read and write to understand life. My dream is to be educated."
Nadia Mustafa, 36.

The classes are held in the neighbourhood where the women live, to make it easier for them to attend, and are taught by teachers from the same area, who have an understanding of the problems women face in their social environment.

(12)

د/م. العز

أنا مش جاهله

"I am not an ignorant person". Dam el-Ezz. She got fed up with her husband's family calling her "ignorant" and wanted to prove them wrong.

# JORDAN
## Dropout Students 2012

My father's death in 2010 in Tyre, southern Lebanon, left my mother alone, as we, her three daughters, had all moved away. Being a Jordanian citizen, she decided to move back to Amman, where her sister lives. My recurrent visits to check on her, in the working-class neighbourhood she took residence in, revealed a particular category of the female population.

They call them "home-bound" students.

As I was looking it up, a conversation with an official from the Ministry of Education revealed that despite the relatively high rate of elementary school enrolment in Jordan, a considerable number of girls drop out in secondary school. They do so for various reasons, but mainly due to the low economic status of their parents. The official couldn't provide an exact number of those who interrupted or ended their schooling, but I couldn't stop wondering what happens to these girls.

Seeking an answer to this question led me to the suburbs of Amman, where the Social Support Centre run by Nihaya Dabdub provides a two-year programme for dropout girls eager to resume their education. The course gives the girls the chance, and the choice, of either continuing high school education or transferring to a technical school. Most choose the latter.

I asked the students: What would be your dream when you finish the programme?

انا بطلت من المدرسة بسبب المعلمات بس كان عندي
امل اني اكمل حلمي افتح اليتيم واصير شرطية
ياترى في امل اني اكمل حلمي :.

"I quit school because of the teachers, but I hope to continue. My dream is to open an orphanage and become a police woman. I wonder if there is hope to fulfil my dream."
Ghadah, 15.

امي اشتغلت في المطار وكانوا اخواني اصغار حتى وكانت اختي اول سنه الها في المدرسة وانا كنت قاعد في البيت بدل امي كنت اغسل واطبخ واشطف البيت كله ،

حلمي هوا اني اصير مهندسة معمار

"My mother had to work at the airport and my siblings were young. I stayed home instead of my mother. I used to wash, cook, and clean the whole house. My dream is to become an architect." Wafa, 16.

برَكـت المدرسه كـان عنـاظمن
وقعـرت فـى الدارسه

كـنـت صـلـه أكـز فـرقـة الوى مدرس
اح آم ~~شـــكـــ~~ زميل
أنا واحي بدنا نفتح صالون

"I left school and stayed home for a year. I would like to specialise in the hotel sector, but my father won't let me. So I will study to become a beautician, and open a salon with my sister."
Rouba, 16.

بجوزني مبكره على النزواج
في أفكار عبير في راس
لبس مش عارفه الحياة لتمشي
معي أو مابمشش معي

"I'm still too young to get married. I have many ideas in mind, but I can't tell whether life will go my way or not." Sabreen, 18.

# YEMEN
Access to Education 2012

In every single report I read in preparation for this project, Yemen was lagging behind on most levels. From large-scale humanitarian crises to political instability, this troubled country has been on a downward spiral for a long time.

As it is the least developed country in the Arab world, access to education is one of the biggest challenges facing girls in Yemen. Two thirds of Yemeni women are illiterate.

My visit to Yemen came after the events, dubbed the Arab Spring, that swept through the region from 2011. The country was left in tatters after the ousting of president Ali Abdullah Saleh, but this was merely a prelude to what would soon degenerate into a civil, and then regional war.

The help of my Yemeni friend, the photographer Boushra Almutawakel, was crucial for this part of the project. She introduced me to Nouria Najm, who runs the Yemen Education and Relief Organization (YERO) providing women with grants to pursue higher education.

Considering that a mere 27% of girls make it to secondary school, I wondered about the rate of those reaching high school or even university. With the help of YERO, I spent three weeks with several women who were the first members in their families to pursue higher education.

I asked them the question: What stood in the way of your education?

احب قراءة قصص الإطفال
عادة والتقليد هما الذي ظلمة المرأه اليمنيه
انا رفض زواج البنه وهي صغيره

"I love reading children's books. I oppose the marriage of girls. Traditions and customs have oppressed Yemeni women." Fayza, 25.

Fayza, the 25-year-old university student from Yemen, was pulled out of school at the age of eight for marriage, only to be divorced a year later. At 14, she became the third wife of a 60-year-old man, who divorced her after she bore him three children. By then she had reached the age of 18. Her older sister persuaded her to finish her education, arguing that this would be her only way to improve her life. In this ultra-conservative society, poverty, the social stigma of divorce, and her parents' opposition made the task extremely difficult. However, that did not dampen Fayza's motivation. In fact, she enrolled in business studies at the university and is currently in her first year.

More women are being trained as teachers since many parents, especially deeply religious ones, will only allow their daughters to be taught by women.

Hanan, 18, decided to study law to contribute to the defence of women in her society who suffer mistreatment. Even though she is the only female student in the class among 22 male classmates, her parents supported her education despite the opposition of some relatives.

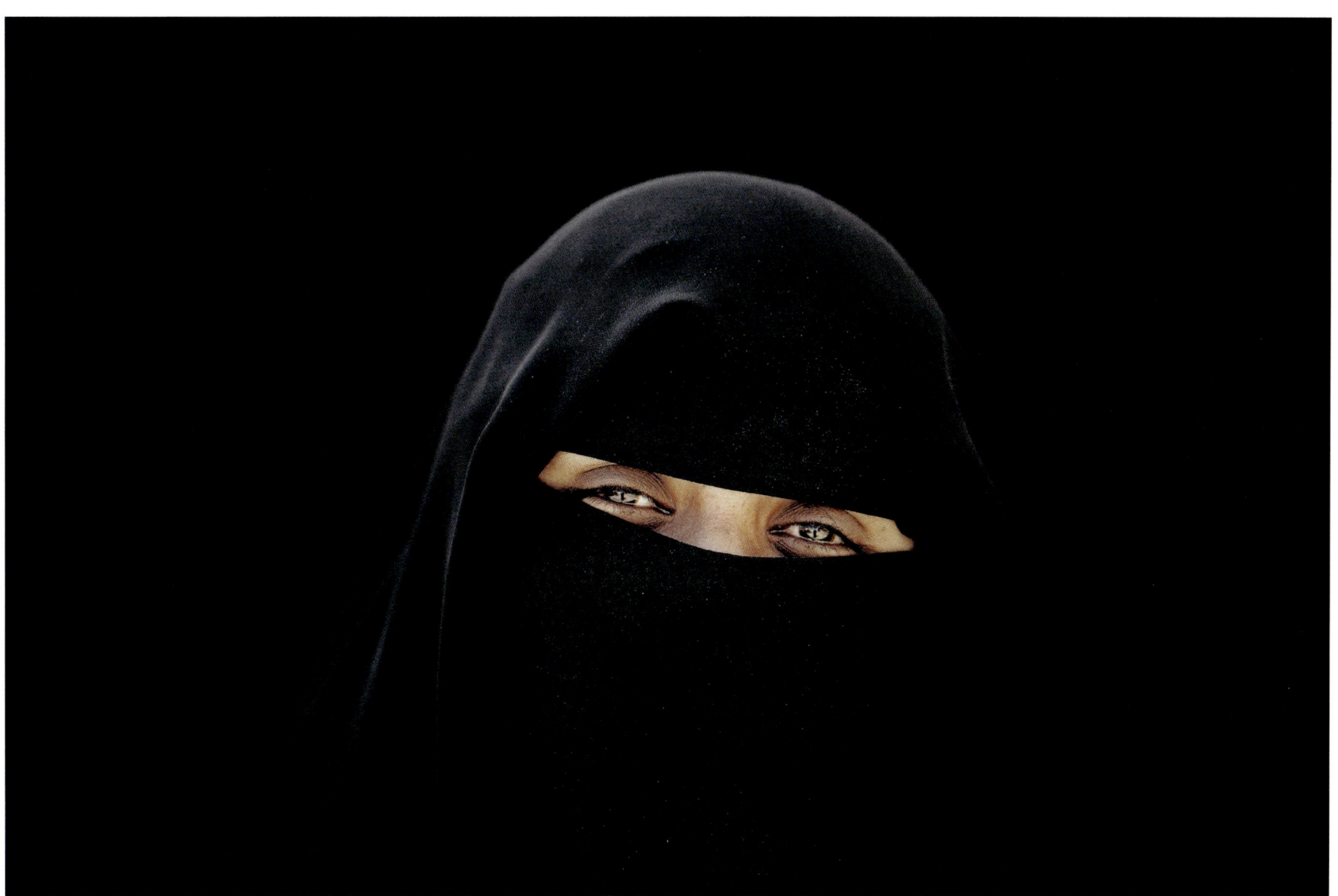

أنا كان طموحي أتخصص علوم سياسية لأنني أعشق السفر
لكن بحكم مجتمعنا لم أحصل على تشجيع فقررت أتخصص علوم مالية
أرغب بأن أتزوج بعد أن أتم تعليمي

"My ambition was to study political science because I love to travel. But because of our society I didn't receive enough support and decided to study finance. I would like to get married after my graduation." Ghadah, 22.

تعلمت من زجل أن أغير نظرة عائلتي نحو تعليم الفتاة حيث
أن نظرتهم هي أن البنت مالها الا الزوج ذو القبر

"I got an education so that I may change the way my family perceives the education of girls. They believe that a girl deserves nothing but marriage or the grave." Khayzaran, 24.

# TUNISIA
## Students' Union 2013

Tunisian women have enjoyed better legal and political status than their counterparts in the rest of the region, particularly secular rights. Under the rule of Habib Bourguiba for three decades, the country witnessed advancement in secular ideas which fuelled the women's emancipation movement.

This has been reflected in the prominent role women played during the revolution which ousted former President Zein El-Abidin Ben Ali in 2011 and ushered in a turbulent period for the entire Arab world.

I arrived in the capital Tunis with the intention of showcasing the power of words used by highly educated, politically engaged women in the post-revolution scene.

I met with activist Fatma Riahi, known as Fatma Arabica, who was frequently arrested during the former regime. She introduced me to four remarkable women studying in different fields at public universities, with whom I spent three weeks.

These university students are politically active, not only within their university campuses, but in their day to day lives.

This took my work in Tunisia in a different direction, compared to the previous countries I visited. I moved out of the classroom to accompany these women in several aspects of their lives. I wanted to see how they hustled to retain their rights under the growing shadow of ultra-conservative Islamists.

The women answered the question: What message would you like to send to young women your age?

نتعلّم مش نغلّم بنتعلّم بنش نتسلّح بحقّسا في الجمود وفي الناس اللّي عملت للفكر حدود نقاوم، والمقاومة انثى نثور، والثورة انثى
نكتب ونبعث الكلام من هن ضفّة لضفّة و نغيّض عيني، ونخلّي الاسلاك الشائكة ورايا

وحلما ونلقاك تقاوم لجنبي

"I learn to teach. I learn to arm myself. To instigate change in people and things that created boundaries of thought. I resist, and resistance is female. I revolt, and revolution is female. I write and send my words out from place to place. I close my eyes and leave the barbed wire behind me, and dream that I meet you standing next to me, resisting." Shams, 21.

Shams, who is studying English literature, won the Student Union elections at her university. She likes to sit with her classmates at their favorite spot, under the graffiti of an image of late Lebanese communist thinker Hassan Hamdan, aka Mahdi Amel, who was assassinated in the 80s. Shams says that Amel's slogans were regularly painted over by Islamist students.

كوني المربية لا على مسلّمات بل على قناعات ، دائمة التساؤل في القناعات
كوني من تريدين لا من يريدونا لا تقبلي استعبادهم
فقد خلقتك أمك حرة كوني المرأة كوني الأم، كوني الأخت
كوني الصديقة كوني للحبيبة العاشقة المتمردة الواعية
قاومي ثوري ابدعي ولا تضعفي كوني أنت فالثورة هي أنت

"Be a teacher of convictions and not maxims, and always question your convictions. Be who you want to be, not who they want you to be. Do not accept their enslavement, for your mother birthed you free. Be the woman. Be the mother. Be the sister. Be the friend. Be the passionate, rebellious, aware lover. Resist, rebel, be creative and do not become weak. Be yourself, for the revolution is you." Yasmine, 22.

Yasmine, a graphic design student, explained that the graffiti on the wall at the public art university says "Paint it again", in defiance of the faculty's administration, which persists in erasing the writings left by students.

غالبا ما أكون أنا ، أينما أكون ... أفعل كلّ شيء بصوت عالي ، أتكلّم ... كلّ ما أدركه أنّي كنت متميّزة في جميع مراحل دراستي ، ولأنّ إنهاء دراستي الجامعيّة وحصولي على عمل جيّد يجعلني قادرة على فكّ الإرتباط مع كلّ من يعرقلني ويحاول أن يجعلني تابعة له .

Khouloud wrote: "Usually, wherever I am, I am myself. I do everything loudly. I speak. I was always exceptional in my studies throughout my schooling. All I know is that finishing my university education and getting a good job will allow me to cut the ties to everyone that hinders me and tries to make me subordinate to them." Khouloud, 21.

Khouloud, an engineering student, often takes part in the weekly demonstrations in front of the Interior Ministry. These demonstrations call for progress in the investigation of the 2013 assassination of opposition leader Chokri Belaid.

Khouloud, who is never reluctant to speak her mind, is often chosen by her classmates to voice issues to the administration on their behalf.

تبدأ الثورة فقط عندما تتمردين على الأنظمة التطيمية الفاسدة القاتلة للفكر.. و الجسد والروح...
...ثوري، فالثورة امرأة

"Revolution starts only when you rebel against the corrupt educational systems that kill intellect, body and soul. Revolt, for the revolution is a woman." Asma, 24.

Asma is a bioengineering student who believes in a secular state, and who is quite active on social media. Regarding her country, she said, "I've always dreamt of discovering a new bacterium. Now, after the revolution, we have a new one every single day." Here Asma refers to the rise of religious fundamentalism in the region, another major obstacle to women in particular.

# SAUDI ARABIA
Women at Work 2016

My project could not have been complete without a visit to Saudi Arabia, a major regional power with a deeply religious and patriarchal society. This oil-rich country's sphere of influence spreads far beyond its borders.

Saudi Arabia has no problem with illiteracy. On the contrary, thousands of women have managed to get government scholarships to study abroad. It has, nevertheless, the highest percentage of female unemployment in the world, due to cultural and religious restrictions.

The Kingdom of Saudi Arabia upholds a strict implementation of Shariah, or Islamic law, which includes male guardianship and strict segregation of the sexes.

While the majority of the employed women are in state teaching jobs, I was intrigued by the type of work the remaining few were able to practise.

I decided to work in Jeddah, a city with a high rate of female unemployment in the kingdom, but also a place known to be relatively less strict in enforcing conservatism than other cities. I spent time with four highly-educated women who allowed me a closer look into their personal and professional lives, and showed me how they managed to bridge the gap between available jobs and their high-level skills.

I asked the women: What does work mean to you?

لا تخف من اختيار تخصص نادر وغريب

ولكن التحدي هو تحقيق هذا الحلم إلى حقيقة

"Don't be afraid to choose a unique major, the challenge is to make this dream a reality."
Alaa, 35.

Alaa is the only certified female ocularist in the whole of the Arab region. With the support of her family, Alaa received her first training course for the profession in Spain. Later in the US, she was training with an American ocularist until September 11, 2001 when she had to interrupt her studies and return to Saudi Arabia due to the non-renewal of her visa. Consequently, she had to wait four years to receive the required Ministry of Health license to open a clinic in 2010 in Jeddah. She refused to leave her country despite the possibility of employment abroad, preferring to provide her expertise to fulfil local needs.

"What will be will be." Ahd, 35.

Filmmaker and actress Ahd left Jeddah at the age of 17 to study law in New York City, but she ended up dropping out of school. Despite some disapproval and everyone's disbelief, including her own, Ahd then studied cinema in NY and pursued it professionally. She came back to Jeddah in 2012 to work on her short film "Sanctity".

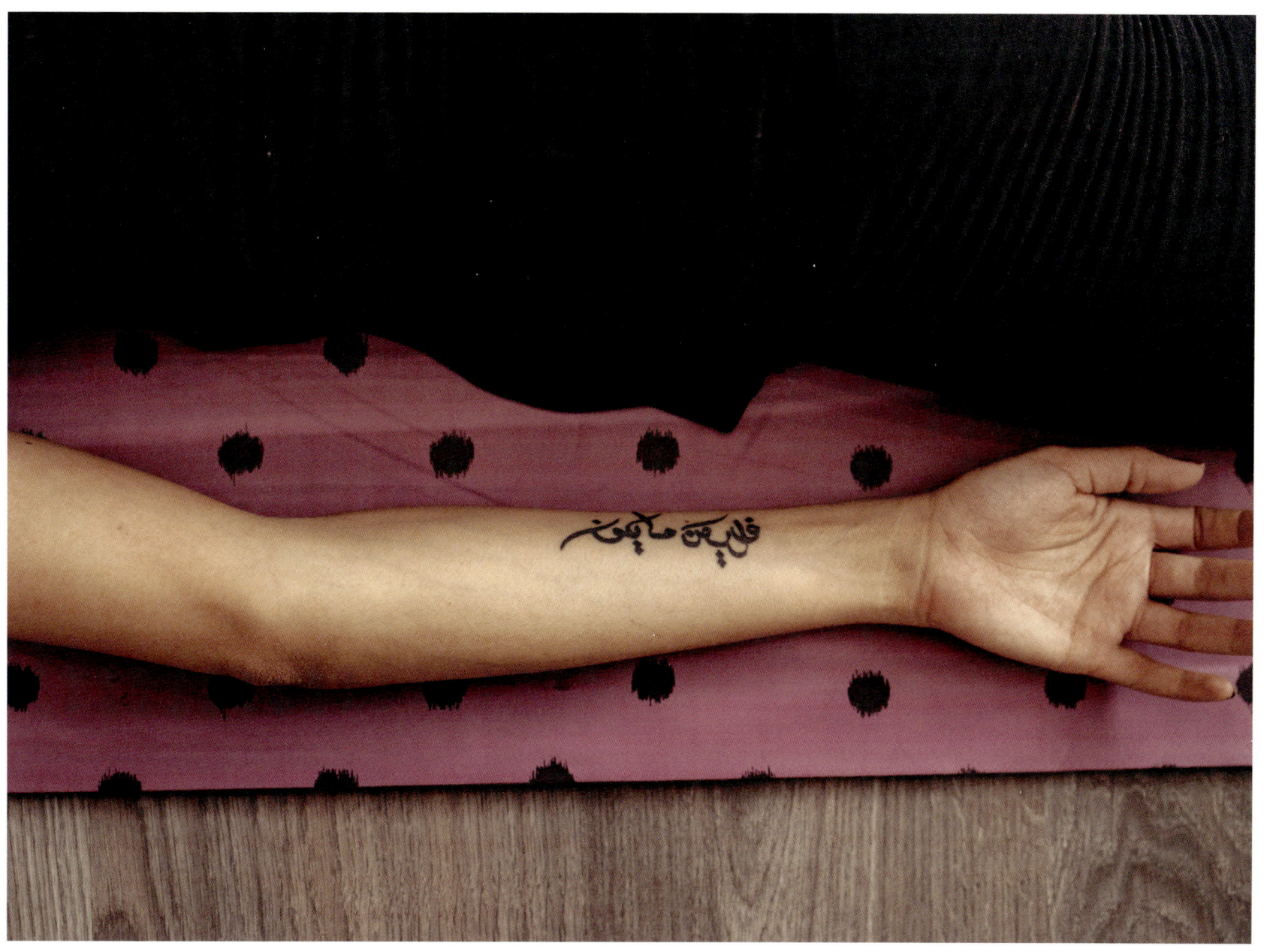

"I don't have to censor myself in front of him", Ahd says of her uncle. "I faced many challenges when I moved back to Saudi. I had to rely on my brothers to get anything done. But I was lucky and many women are not. It got me thinking what would a woman do without a man in her life."

"My observation and fascination with stories started at an early age. Watching my grandmother Sarah, the greatest warrior and storyteller, relate her tales was riveting. She was animated, timed and very funny. Her infectious laugh is what got me."

أعمل في مجال التعليم لأنه الاستثمار المطلوب لمستقبل بلادي

"I work in the education sector, because it's the needed investment for the future of my country." Basma, 32.

Basma is the Managing Director of Training and one of three women who co-founded Emkan Education, a pedagogical advisory and school development company based in Jeddah. It provides education advisory services to private and public institutions, and specialises in developing curricula and customising educational content.

عَمَلي هُوَ حَياتي، وَحَياتي هِيَ عَمَلي

"My work is my life and my life is my work." Rozana, 32.

Rozana is one of the first Saudi woman to be an Associate Certified Coach and Certified Professional CoActive Coach. Most of her work is centred on creating opportunities for people to live a more purposeful life and to help them lean into impactful leadership. Currently, she is working with a number of organisations led by Saudi women.

"I think of it every single day – the blessing of a good, kind-hearted husband, who is my best friend. I really appreciate our relationship and his supportive role."

# **GAZA**
Blockade 2016

Among the universal basic human rights, the right to education and to freedom of movement are particularly important for me. In Gaza, most people are deprived of both.

The Gaza Strip has been under Israeli occupation since 1967. In mid-2007, the Islamic Resistance Movement, or Hamas, won a majority in the Legislative Council elections, and took full control of the coastal strip. With the already shaky balance of power among Palestinians gone, Israel imposed a strict air, land, and sea blockade on the territory, citing security concerns.

For the UN's Office for the Coordination of Humanitarian Affairs (OCHA), the ongoing siege "undermines the living conditions in the coastal enclave" while fragmenting "its economic and social fabric", a phenomenon aggravated by Egyptian restrictions on Rafah, Gaza's sole crossing point with Egypt on its southern border. As a result, basic educational services, among many others, have severely deteriorated. Higher education is extremely limited and lacks many disciplines. Consequently, many students seek to further their education abroad.

My focus in Gaza was on Palestinian women whose ambitions of academic enhancement abroad are in limbo due to harsh and unjustified travel restrictions.

My attention was drawn to this category during a chat with a friend at a coffee shop in Amman. My friend was from Gaza, but she was stuck in the Jordanian capital while waiting to receive a place at a university in the UK.

The Israeli blockade restricts freedom of movement for Gaza residents, preventing many students from pursuing higher education abroad. Leaving the enclave requires getting to Egypt or Jordan, via one of the border crossings, after a lengthy process to obtain multiple travel permits.

Many aspiring students have to wait for months to get an exit permit. Many others have their applications rejected, and thus end up losing their scholarships.

During my stay in Gaza, I met four women dealing with the complicated process of getting travel permits. Their stories reflect how they patiently dealt with the uncertainty of their situation in a place that barely has time to breathe between wars, and how they handled the anxiety and anguish inherent in these unpredictable procedures.

I asked them: Why is it important to continue your education?

وأنتي صغيرة رح يركبولك
جناحات ويحكولك إنك حرة! وبس
تكبري رح يقصوا هالجناحات ويحطوكي
بقفص العادة والعيب ..
قررت أسافر لإني حرة،

"When you're young, they'll give you wings and say you are free, but when you grow up, they'll cut off those wings and put you in the cage of traditions and shame. I decided to travel because I'm free. And my right to decide my destiny is a personal issue." Asma, 21.

Asma's friends, who were leaving Gaza for the first time, were allowed to stay in Jerusalem for less than a day, to receive visas to attend a six-week leadership training course in the US. She, on the other hand, was denied a travel permit.

After being accepted to study English literature at a university in the US, Asma has been trying for over a year to leave Gaza through one of its two official border-crossings.

In addition to her frustration with the travel permit refusal, Asma's family is putting pressure on her to get married and stay in Gaza, but Asma believes she's too young to get married. She wants to finish her studies first.

Sally, 18, got accepted to study medicine in Germany and would like to specialise in surgery. Her visa to Germany is ready, and after her travel permit from Jordan got refused three times, her dad managed to add her name on a list to be able to travel through Rafah. On that day Sally packed her things and went to the border without being sure whether she would be able to cross or not. She had to wait for over 9 hours before she was allowed to go through to the Egyptian side of the border. She ended up spending the night sleeping on the floor and took a minivan the following day heading to Cairo.

أكبر مواجهة بحياتي هيا أني هببيت تعزفن عود من غزه     كانت مواجهة صعبة ونحنوا
تحدي بيني وبين نفسي ولحتى الان بواجه محيطي وكله بشكل أمل ولكنه لسا بحبس العود من بوضوع
تبلاحمضن سوا بالموسيقى والعزف او بالسفر

"The biggest challenge I faced in my life was being a woman playing the oud in Gaza. The difficulty increased as I was actually challenging myself as well. I'm still up to this moment confronting the whole of society, and am subjected to restrictions when it comes to music and travel." Reem, 26.

Reem is the only female member in her band, and was recently banned by the Hamas government from performing in public.

"Gaza is a very conservative place, and the oud instrument is seen as a masculine one, that's why it's rare to find a woman playing the oud, as if it were something bad. This fact made me even more determined to learn the oud, and my mother was always supportive about my passion for music."

Reem volunteers with Tamer Institute for Community Education in Gaza. The foundation turned a minibus into a mobile library and tours different areas in Gaza to encourage kids to read.

"Unemployment is high in Gaza and it's hard to find jobs. During the last war on Gaza, I played music to people taking shelter in schools to ease their fear. After the war I gave music classes to women to help them cope with the trauma of the war."

During power cuts at night, Reem relies on her smart phone light, sits in her living room, and plays the oud.

"We're under lots of pressure on all fronts. In addition to our restriction of movement, there is enormous social pressure on women. I only wear the hijab when I go outside because it's expected of me to do so. That's why when I get upset I play music. Music is my life."

علشان ما بدي أعيش تحت سيطرة أي زلمة بالعالم. بدي أعيش مع شريك مش مع ولي أمر. علشان هيك لازم أتعلم.. أتعلم أكون مستقلة وحرة...

"Because I don't want to live under the control of any man. I want a partner not a male guardian. This is why I want to be educated. To learn how to be free and independent."
Abeer, 29.

"I was 20 when the blockade started. It's been nine years now. And I've survived three wars in less than six years."

Abeer is a journalist who works for different publications.

"I'm 29 years old and still single. By local standards that's late. In my case, because I work and I'm financially independent, it's hard for a man to get the approval of his family to marry me. I'm seen as someone who can't even make a cup of coffee, they'd say 'she's liberal, not like our girls'."

كتبت أسماء (٢١ عاماً) «وانتي صغيرة يركبولك جناحات ويحكولك انك حرّة وبس تكبري رح يقصوا هالجناحات ويحطوكي بقفص العادة والعيب...قررت أسافر لأني حرة وحقي في تقرير مصيري حاجة خاصة». (صفحة 116)

أجيز لأصدقاء أسماء، الذين يغادرون غزة للمرّة الأولى، المكوث في القدس أقلّ من ٢٤ ساعة للحصول على تأشيرات دخول إلى الولايات المتحدة لحضور دورة تدريب لستة أشهر. لكن رخصة سفر أسماء رفضت مجدداً. بعد قبولها في جامعة أميركية لدراسة الأدب الإنكليزي، حاولت أسماء طوال عام مغادرة القطاع بلا جدوى. (صفحة 119)

إلى جانب شعور أسماء بالإحباط بسبب رفض منحها رخصة السفر، تُضاعف عائلتها الضغط عليها كي تتزوّج وتبقى في غزة. لكن أسماء ترى أنها ما زالت صغيرة على الزواج، وتريد أنهاء دروسها أوّلاً. (صفحة 123)

قُبل طلب سالي (١٨ عاما) لدراسة الطب في ألمانيا، وهي تريد التخصّص في الجراحة. بعد حصولها على تأشيرة ألمانية رفضت سلطات الأردن  ثلاث مرات منحها «عدم ممانعة»، قبل أن يتمكن والدها من إدراج اسمها على لائحة أتاحت لها المغادرة من معبر رفح. في ذاك اليوم وضّبت سالي حقائبها واتجهت إلى رفح بلا أي ضمانة بأنها ستتمكن من المغادرة. انتظرت عند المعبر أكثر من تسع ساعات قبل أن يؤذن لها بالانتقال إلى الشطر المصري من المعبر، وأضطرّت في النهاية إلى افتراش الأرض ليلاً قبل ان تستقل حافلة في اليوم التالي إلى القاهرة. (صفحة 125)

كتبت ريم (٢٦ عاماً) «أكبر مواجهة بحياتي إني صبيّة بتعزف عود بغزة. كانت مواجهة صعبة وفيها تحدي بيني وبين نفسي. ولحتى الآن بواجه مجتمع ولكن بشكل أقل، ولكن في بعض القيود في الموضوع بتلاحقني سواء بالموسيقى والعزف أو بالسفر». (صفحة 128)

ريم هي الفتاة الوحيدة في فرقتها، ومؤخّراً منعتها حكومة حماس من الأداء أمام الجمهور. «غزة محافظة جدّاً، والعود يعتبر أداة يعزفها الرجال، لذلك من النادر العثور على عازفة عود، وكأنها أمر سيئ. هذا ضاعف من تصميمي على تعلّم العود، ولطالما دعمَت والدتي شغفي بالموسيقى». (صفحة 131)

ريم تلعب مع الأطفال أثناء تطوّعها في «مؤسسة تامر للتعليم المجتمعي» في غزة. حوّلت المؤسّسةُ حافلةً إلى مكتبةٍ جوّالةٍ تزور مختلف مناطق القطاع لتشجيع الأطفال على القراءة. «البطالة مرتفعة في غزة، ويصعب العثور على وظائف. أثناء الحرب الأخيرة على غزة 2014 عزفتُ الموسيقى للاجئين في المدارس للتخفيف من خوفهم. بعد الحرب أعطيت دروساً في الموسيقى للنساء لمساعدتهن على التعامل مع صدمة الحرب». (صفحة 133)

أثناء انقطاع الكهرباء ليلاً تعتمد ريم على ضوء هاتفها الجوال لتعزف العود في غرفة الجلوس في منزلها. «نتعرض لضغط كبير من جميع الاتجاهات. وبالإضافة إلى تقييد حركتنا هناك ضغوط اجتماعية هائلة على النساء. أضع الحجاب فقط عندما أخرج لأن الأمر متوقّع منّي. لهذا أعزف عندما أشعر بالاستياء. الموسيقى حياتي». (صفحة 135)

كتبت عبير (٢٩ عاماً) «علشان ما بدي أعيش تحت سيطرة أي زلمة بالعالم بدي أعيش مع شريك مش مع وليّ أمر...علشان هيك لازم أتعلّم، اتعلّم أكون مستقلّة وحرّة». (صفحة 136)

«كنت في العشرين من العمر عند بدء الحصار، ومرّت تسع سنوات. نجوت من ثلاثة حروب في أقلّ من ست سنوات». (صفحة 139)

«انا في الـ ٢٩ وما زلت عزباء، وهذه سن متقدّمة بحسب المعايير المحلية. في حالتي، لأني أعمل ولأنني مستقلة ماديًا، من الصعب على رجل أن ينال موافقة عائلته على الزواج بي. فهنا يعتبرون انني عاجزة عن إعداد فنجان من القهوة، يقولون متحرّرة، مش متل بناتنا». (صفحة 141)

# غزة
## الخاتمة ٢٠١٦

بين حقوق الإنسان الأساسية، يشكل الحق في التعلّم وحرية التحرك أولوية بالنسبة لي. وسكّان غزة بأغلبيتهم محرومون من كليهما.

خضع قطاع غزة للاحتلال الاسرائيلي منذ ١٩٦٧. في منتصف ٢٠٠٧ سيطرت «حركة المقاومة الإسلامية - حماس» على القطاع الساحلي، بعد حرب طاحنة مع «حركة فتح» بزعامة الرئيس الفلسطيني محمود عباس. ومع انهيار توازن القوى الهش أصلاً بين المعسكرين الفلسطينيين، سارعت إسرائيل لفرض حصار بري وبحري وجوّي على القطاع، عَزَته إلى دواع أمنية.

اعتبر مكتب الأمم المتحدة لتنسيق الشؤون الإنسانية أن الحصار الذي ما زال قائماً «يقوّض ظروف المعيشة في الجيب الساحلي» ويفتت «نسيجه الاقتصادي والاجتماعي». وما يضاعف ذلك، القيودُ التي تفرضها السلطات المصرية على معبر رفح، المعبر الوحيد للقطاع مع مصر على حدوده الجنوبية. بالتالي شهدت الخدمات التعليمية الأولية، بين قطاعات كثيرة أخرى، تدهوراً هائلاً، فيما التعليم العالي محدود جدّاً وتنقصه اختصاصات كثيرة. لذلك يحاول العديد من الطلاب متابعة دراستهم في الخارج.

ركّزتُ في غزّة على الفلسطينيات اللواتي اضطررن إلى تعليق طموحاتهنّ في متابعة العلم في الخارج بسبب قيود مشدّدة غير مبرّرة على سفرهنّ.

علمت بهذه الظاهرة للمرة الأولى أثناء حديث مع صديقة غزّاوية في أحد مقاهي عمّان، حيث روت لي أنها تنتظر في العاصمة الأردنية وصول رسالة قبولها في جامعة بريطانية. المشكلة أنها جازفت بمغادرة القطاع عندما سنحت لها فرصة نادرة للخروج، دون أن تعلم متى تصل الرسالة، هذا إن كانت ستصل.

أما مغادرة القطاع المُحاصر، فليست بالأمر السهل وتتطلب الوصول إلى مصر أو الأردن، وهذا رهن بالحصول على رخص «عدم ممانعة» متعدّدة، إسرائيلية وأردنية أو مصرية، بحسب معبر المغادرة المعني.

لذلك يضطر الكثيرون من الطلاب الطموحين إلى الانتظار لأشهر طويلة من أجل الحصول على رخصة خروج، فيما تُرفَض طلبات كثيرين منهم فيخسرون مِنحَهم الجامعية.

في غزة تعرّفت إلى أربع شابات يواجهن صعوبات في الحصول على رخص الخروج. وتعكس قصصهنّ كيف تسلّحن بالصبر للتعامل مع غموض وضعهن، وواجهن القلق والتوتر الناجمين عنه في القطاع الذي لا يتسنى له التقاط انفاسه بين حرب وأخرى.

سألت كلا منهن «ما أهمّية متابعة تعليمك؟»

كتبت آلاء على صورتها «لا تخافي من اختيار تخصص نادر وغريب، ولكن التحدي هو تحقيق هذا الحلم إلى حقيقة». (صفحة 84)

آلاء هي الأخصائية الأولى في العيون الصناعية في السعودية، لذلك استغرق الأمر أربع سنوات حتّى تحصل على رخصة من وزارة الصحة وتفتح عيادة في ٢٠١٠. وفيما بذلَت جهوداً حثيثة ومتكررة لإثبات الحاجة إلى هذا الاختصاص، رفضت مغادرة بلدها رغم فرص العمل في الخارج، مفضلة تكريس خبرتها لحاجاته. (صفحة 87)

كتبت عهد: «فليكن ما يكون» (صفحة 90)

غادرت عهد جدة عندما كانت في عامها السابع عشر لدراسة الحقوق في نيويورك، لكنها لم تكمل هذا التخصص، وفضّلت دراسة السينما وامتهانها رغم معارضة البعض. في ٢٠١٢ عادت إلى جدة للعمل على فيلمها القصير «حرمة» (صفحة 93)

تقول عهد عن خالها «لست مضطرة لممارسة أي رقابة ذاتية بوجوده»، «واجهت تحديات كثيرة بعد عودتي إلى السعودية واضطررت إلى الاعتماد على أشقائي لإتمام أي عمل. لكنني محظوظة، على عكس نساء كثيرات، ولطالما تساءلت كيف يدبرن أمورهن بلا رجل في حياتهن. (صفحة 97)

«بدأ شغفي بالقصص في سن مبكّر، عبر جدتي سارة، أروع مناضلة وراوية أعرفها. شاهدتها تروي القصص بشغف مذهل. كانت تلونها وتوقّتها وتطعّمها بالفكاهة، وضحكتها المعدية هي ما تعلّقت به. رغم معاناتها من مآسٍ كثيرة، انطبعت في مخيّلتها بصور جميلة ودرامية ومضحكة. هذه الشخصيات والمشاهد الحيّة التي وصفتها خلّفت أثراً في مخيلتي وأثارت عواطفي. وسرعان ما تعلّقت بهذه العاطفة التي تثيرها رواية مثيرة داخل المرء، بلطف وعمق معاً. أردت، أنا أيضاً، أن استكشف كيف يمكنني أن أروي قصصاً تحرّك المشاعر». (صفحة 99)

كتبت بسمة «أعمل في مجال التعليم لأنه الاستثمار المطلوب لمستقبل بلادي». (صفحة 100)

تدير بسمة فرع التدريب في شركة «إمكان التعليمية»، التي توفّر استشارات لتطوير المدارس والتعليم، والتي شاركت في تأسيسها مع سيّدتين أخريين في جدة. وتتعامل الشركة مع مؤسسات خاصة وعامة، وتتخصص في بلورة المناهج وتكييف المضمون التعليمي المفصل حسب الطلب. (صفحة 103)

كتبت روزانا «عملي هو حياتي وحياتي هي عملي». (صفحة 106)

روزانا هي احدى السعوديات الأُوَل في استحصال رخصة مدرّبة شخصيّة محترفة. يتمحور الجزء الأكبر من عملها حول فتح الفرص كي يعيش الأفراد حياة هادفة ومساعدتهم للتمتع بقدرة على القيادة تساعدهم على النهوض، وهي تتعاون حالياً مع عدد من الجمعيات التي تديرها سعوديات. (صفحة 109)

قالت روزانا «أفكّر بذلك كل يوم، النعمة المتمثّلة بزوج طيّب حنون هو صديقي الحميم. أقدّر كثيراً علاقتنا ودوره الداعم». (صفحة 111)

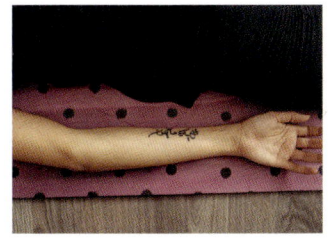

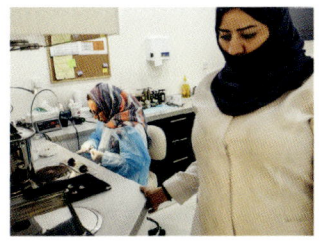
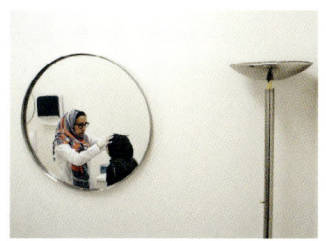

## السعودية
نساء عاملات ٢٠١٦

لا يكتمل مشروع كهذا بلا محطة في السعودية، المملكة الخليجية الكبرى التي لطالما شكّلت قطباً سياسياً واقتصادياً ودينياً واسع التأثير في المنطقة العربية وأبعد.

لا تطرح الأمية مشكلة بارزة في السعودية، بل على العكس حصلت آلاف الشابات على مِنحٍ حكومية للدراسة في الخارج.

في المقابل تسجّل السعودية النسبة الأعلى عالمياً لبطالة النساء بسبب القيود الاجتماعية والدينية.

تجد نسبة ٩٦٪ من النساء العاملات وظائف في التعليم الرسمي، ما أثار فضولي بشأن نسبة ٤٪ المتبقية.

قررت العمل في مدينة جدة التي تسجل نسب بطالة مرتفعة في المملكة، وتعتبر نسبيّاً أقل تشدّداً من سائر المدن الكبرى في تطبيق الأنظمة المحافظة. أمضيت الوقت مع اربع نساء تلقين تعليماً عالياً، فتمكّنتُ من معايشتهنّ في حياتهن الخاصة وعملهن وأفكارهن واطّلعتُ على ما فعلن لتجاوز الثغرة بين الوظائف المتاحة وكفاءاتهن الرفيعة.

أردت أن توضح كلّ منهن لي «ماذا يعني لك عملك؟»

كتبت شمس «نتعلم بش (لكي) نعلّم، نتعلّم بش نتسلّح نعقّس في الجمود وفي الناس الي عملت للفكر حدود ونقاوم والمقاومة أنثى، ثوّر والثورة أنثى نكتب ونبعث الكلام من ضفة لضفة ونغمّض عيني ونخلّي الأسلاك الشائكة ورايا ونحلم ونلقاك تقاوم بجنبي». (صفحة 60)

فازت شمس، طالبة الأدب الإنكليزي، في انتخابات اتحاد الطلاب في جامعتها. وهي تحب الجلوس مع زملائها في ركنهم المفضل، تحت رسم جداري كبير يصوّر المفكر اللبناني الراحل حسن حمدان المعروف باسم مهدي عامل، الذي اغتيل في الثمانينيات. وأفادت شمس أن الطلاب الاسلاميين يغطون باستمرار شعارات عامل المخطوطة على الجدران بالطلاء الابيض. (صفحة 63)

كتبت ياسمين «كوني المربّية لا على مسلّمات بل على قناعات، دائمة التساؤل عن القناعات. كوني من تريدين لا من يريدون، لا تقبلي استعبادهم فقد خلقتك أمك حرة كوني المرأة كوني الأم كوني الأخت كوني الصديقة كوني الحبيبة العاشقة المتمرّدة الواعية. قاومي ثوري أبدعي ولا تضعفي كوني أنت فالثورة هي أنت». (صفحة 66)

ياسمين، الطالبة في التصميم الغرافيكي، تحادث زملاءها في كلية الفنون بتونس، أمام جدار يعبّر الطلاب عليه بالشعارات عن تحدي إدارة الجامعة التي تواصل محو كتاباتهم. (صفحة 69)

كتبت خلود «غالبا ما أكون أنا، أينما أكون...أفعل كلّ شيء بصوت عال، أتكلّم...كلّ ما أعرفه أنني كنت متميّزة في جميع مراحل دراستي، ولأن إنهاء دراستي الجامعية وحصولي على عمل جيّد يجعلني قادرة على فكّ الارتباط مع كلّ من يعرقلني ويحاول ان يجعلني تابعة له». (صفحة 72)

خلود التي تدرس الهندسة تهتف أثناء تظاهرة أسبوعية أمام وزارة الداخلية للمطالبة بإحراز تقدم في التحقيقات في اغتيال المعارض اليساري شكري بلعيد عام 2013. (صفحة 75)

خلود تتفاوض مع أستاذة اللغة الإنكليزية على تعديل توقيت الامتحان المقبل. غالباً ما ينتدب الزملاء خلود لتمثيلهم في طرح مطالبهم على الإدارة. (صفحة 77)

كتبت أسماء «تبدأ الثورة فقط عندما تتمردين على الأنظمة التعليمية الفاسدة القاتلة للفكر... والجسد والروح... ثوري، فالثورة امرأة». (صفحة 78)

تنشط أسماء، طالبة الهندسة الحيوية، على مواقع التواصل وهي من مؤيدي علمانية الدولة. في حديث عن بلدها قالت «لطالما حلمت باكتشاف جرثومة جديدة. لكننا الآن بعد الثورة نكتشف جرثومة جديدة كل يوم»، في إشارة الى تصاعد التشدد الإسلامي في المنطقة الذي يشكل عقبة إضافية أمام النساء خصوصاً. (صفحة 81)

## تونس
### اتحاد الطلاب ٢٠١٣

لطالما تمتعت التونسيات بوضع قانوني وسياسي أفضل من سائر النساء العربيّات، خصوصاً على مستوى الحقوق المدنية. فأثناء حكم الحبيب بورقيبة لثلاثة عقود شهد البلد تقدماً على مستوى الحقوق المدنية عزّز حركة تحرّر المرأة.

انعكس ذلك في الدور الذي لعبته التونسيات في الثورة التي أطاحت بحكم زين العابدين بن علي في ٢٠١١، وشكّلت انطلاقة مرحلة من الاضطرابات والثورات عمّت المنطقة العربية.

وصلتُ إلى العاصمة التونسية بهدف تسليط الضوء على قوة الكلمات التي استخدمتها ناشطات ملتزمات سياسياً تلقين تعليماً عالياً في مشهد ما بعد الثورة.

بعد لقائي مع الناشطة فاطمة رياحي صاحبة مدوّنة «فاطمة ارابيكا» التي نالت نصيبها من الاعتقالات أثناء الحكم السابق بسبب تعليقاتها السياسية الناقدة، عرّفتني إلى أربع نساء مميّزات يدرسن مجالات مختلفة في الجامعات الرسمية، أمضيت برفقتهن ثلاثة أسابيع.

هؤلاء الطالبات ناشطات سياسياً ضمن جامعاتهنّ كما في حياتهن اليومية.

على ضوء معايشتي لهنّ، أخذ عملي في تونس اتجاهاً مختلفاً مقارنة بالبلدان السابقة التي زرتها. فقد خرجتُ من الصف ورافقت الشابات في حياتهنّ اليوميّة. أردت التعرّف إلى كفاحهنّ من أجل الدفاع عن حقوقهن في ظل تنامي النفوذ الاسلامي المتشدد.

أجابت كل من الناشطات على السؤال التالي «ما الرسالة التي تريدين توجيهها إلى الفتيات من جيلك؟»

كتبت فايزة «أحبّ قراءة قصص الأطفال. أنا أرفض زواج البنت وهي صغيرة. العادات والتقاليد هي التي ظلمت المرأة اليمنية». (صفحة 41)

فايزة طالبة جامعية يمنية في الـ25 من العمر. في سن الثامنة تركت المدرسة للزواج لكنها طُلّقت بعد عام. في سن الـ14 باتت الزوجة الثالثة لستينيّ، ولدت منه ثلاثة أطفال، قبل طلاقها مجدداً في سن الـ18. لاحقاً أقنعتها شقيقتها الكبرى بإتمام الدراسة لقناعتها انها الطريقة الوحيدة لتحسين حياتها. ورغم تشدد مجتمعها والفقر والوصمة التي تلحق بالنساء المطلقات ومعارضة والديها لاستئنافها الدراسة، لم تثبط عزيمة فايزة، وتسجلت لدراسة إدارة الأعمال في الجامعة حيث كانت تتابع سنتها الدراسية الأولى. (صفحة 43)

يجري تدريب عدد متزايد من الفتيات على التعليم، لرفض نسبة كبيرة من الأهل، لا سيما الأكثر تشدداً، تلقي بناتهنّ العلم إلا من معلّمة. (صفحة 47)

قررت حنان (18 عاماً) دراسة الحقوق لأنها أرادت المساهمة في الدفاع عن نساء مجتمعها من أي سوء معاملة. ودعم والداها تعليمها رغم أنها الفتاة الوحيدة بين 22 زميلاً، وسط اعتراض عدد من الأقارب. (صفحة 51)

كتبت وجدان «أنا وجدان، أمنيتي أن أكون أستاذة من أجل أن أعلّم الأطفال». (صفحة 52)

كتبت عائشة (33 عاماً) على صورتها «تعلمت حتى لا أعتمد على الرجل بكل شيء وأحس باستقلاليتي». (صفحة 53)

كتبت غادة «أنا كان طموحي أتخصص علوم سياسية لأني أعشق السفر. لكن بحكم مجتمعنا لم أحصل على تشجيع فقررت أتسجّل علوم ماليّة. أرغب أن أتزوّج بعد أن أتمّ تعليمي». (صفحة 55)

كتبت خيزران «تعلمت من أجل أن أغيّر نظرة عائلتي نحو تعليم الفتاة حيث أن نظرتهم هي أن البنت مالها إلا الزوج او القبر». (صفحة 57)

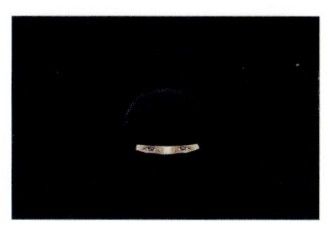

## اليمن
### الحصول على فرص التعلّم ٢٠١٢

في كل تقرير قرأته في التحضير لهذا المشروع ورد اليمن في أدنى مراتب التصنيفات المختلفة، من الأزمات الانسانية الواسعة النطاق إلى النزاعات المسلحة، مروراً بحقوق الانسان ومستوى التعليم.

في هذا البلد الأكثر فقراً في العالم العربي، تبلغ نسبة النساء الأميات الثلثين، وتعتبر فرص التعلّم من أكبر التحديات التي تواجه الفتيات.

زرت اليمن في أعقاب أحداث «الربيع العربي»، في فترة توتر حاد أعقبت الإطاحة بالنظام السابق برئاسة علي عبد الله صالح، وشكلت مقدمة لحرب أهلية ثم إقليمية.

بمساعدة حيويّة من صديقتي اليمنية المصوّرة الفوتوغرافية بشرى المتوكل، التقيت نورية نجم، مديرة «منظمة التعليم والإغاثة اليمنية» التي تقدّم منحاً دراسية للنساء تجيز لهنّ متابعة دراسات عليا.

أردت معرفة المزيد بشأن نسبة النساء اللواتي يتمكّن من اختتام الدراسة الثانوية أو الجامعية، بعدما علمت أن ٢٧٪ فحسب يصلن إلى المرحلة الثانوية. وأتاحت لي المنظمة تمضية ثلاثة أسابيع برفقة عدد من النساء اللواتي كنّ أول من تابع دراسات عليا في عائلاتهن.

طرحت على كلّ منهن السؤال التالي: «ما الذي عرقل متابعة دراستك؟»

كتبت ربى (١٦ عاماً) «تركت المدرسة ... كنت حابه آخذ فندقية أبوي عارض. رح آخد تجميل ...أنا وأختي بدنا نفتح صالون». (صفحة 33)

كتبت صابرين (١٨ عاماً) «بعدني صغيرة على الزواج. في أفكار كثير في راسي ، بس مش عارفه الحياة تمشي معي أو ما تمشي معي». (صفحة 35)

كتبت غادة (١٥ عاماً) «أنا بطلت من المدرسة بسبب المعلمات بس كان عندي أمل أكمل. حلمي أفتح الميتم وصير شرطية. يا ترى في أمل اني كمل حلمي». (صفحة 29)

كتبت وفاء (١٦ عاماً) «إمي اشتغلت في المطار وكانوا إخواني صغار كتير وكانت أختي أول سنه إلها في المدرسة وأنا كنت قاعد في البيت بدل إمي كنت اغسل واطبخ واشطف البيت كلو. حلمي هو إني اصير مهندسة معمار». (صفحة 31)

 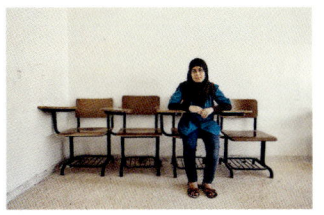   

## الأردن
### جليسات المنازل ٢٠١٢

بعد وفاة والدي عام ٢٠١٠ في صور، جنوب لبنان، قرّرت والدتي التي تحمل الجنسية الأردنية الإقامة في عمان، قرب شقيقتها. في زياراتي المتكرّرة إليها في الحي الشعبي الذي اتخذت فيه منزلاً، أثارت انتباهي ظاهرة خاصة بين الفتيات.

يطلقون عليهنّ تسمية «جليسات المنازل»، أي الفتيات اللواتي ينقطعن عن الدراسة.

أثناء البحث عن هذه الظاهرة أطلعني مسؤول في وزارة التربية أنه رغم نسبة التسجيل المرتفعة في المدارس الابتدائية في الأردن، ما زال عدد الفتيات اللواتي يقطعن الدراسة لمختلف الدوافع مرتفعاً. أضاف ان ذلك يحدث خصوصاً مع حلول المرحلة الثانوية، لكن تعذر عليه تحديد نسبة دقيقة. هذه المعلومات ضاعفت فضولي بشأن مصير تلك الفتيات.

أتاح لي التعاون مع «مركز الدعم الاجتماعي»، آنذاك بإدارة نهاية دبدوب، إمضاء الوقت برفقة عدد من الفتيات في ضواحي عمان. فالمركز يوفر برنامجاً دراسياً من عامين للفتيات اللواتي قطعن الدراسة، يسمح لهن مواصلة التعلّم في الثانوية أو في مدرسة مهنية. وغالباً ما تختار الفتيات المسار الثاني.

سألت الطالبات « بِمَ تحلمن بعد اختتام البرنامج؟»

خطّت نادية أوّل كلمتين تعلَّمت كتابتهما، «من أنا». قررت نادية التسجّل في دروس محو الأمية بعدما ضاقت ذرعاً بمشاهدة فيديوهات موسيقى «البوب» العربية على التلفزيون. كما أنها تريد التمكن من قراءة الصحيفة. (صفحة 13)

كتبت إجلال معوّض (53 عاماً) «تركت المدرسة من أربعين سنة. حصل موقف صعب، كان لازم أساعد ابني في المدرسة واكتب شكوى وما عرفتش، فكان الموقف صعب ومحرج، فصممت أتعلّم عشان أقرأ واكتب. من غير علم ظلام، إذا أشوف كتابة ومش عارفة أقرأ وكأني مش شايفة. في الأول زوجي عرضها (عارضها) عشان مش عايز أخرُج. وبعدما أنا صممت إني أتعلّم نفسيتي اتحسنت». (صفحة 15)

كتبت سناء السيد (31 عاما) «نفسي أتعلم عشان المواصلات لأني بتوه». وغالباً ما يرافقها ابنها الأصغر أيمن الذي يبلغ الرابعة من العمر إلى الحصص. (صفحة 19)

كتبت نادية مصطفى (36 عاما) «عايزة اتعلم عشان أفهم الدنيا. حلمي أتعلم». (صفحة 21)

تُنظَّم الحصص في الحي الذي تقيم فيه النسوة كي يتمكّن من الحضور، وتعطي الدروس معلّمات من المنطقة نفسها، لإدراكهن المشاكل التي تواجهها ربات المنزل في بيئتهن الاجتماعية. (صفحة 23)

خطّت دام العز على صورتها «أنا مش جاهلة»، وسعت إلى تعلّم القراءة بعدما سئمت من سماع عائلة زوجها تنتقدها لأنها «جاهلة»، كي تثبت خطأهم. (صفحة 25)

## مصر
### دروس محو الأمية ٢٠٠٩

غمرني شعور بالإلفة فيما انحرفت سيارة الأجرة بحدّة لتفادي مئات العربات الأخرى في طريقها، في سلوك معهود على طرقات القاهرة المكتظة. شعرت أنني خظوت إلى العالم المألوف لمئات الأفلام والأغاني والروايات التي طعّمَت يوميات الملايين مثلي في المنطقة. اعتباراً من منتصف القرن التاسع عشر أصبحت «أم الدنيا» قطباً لهواة مختلف الفنون والآداب ومحترفيها الذين أتوا طمعاً بذرّات من إشعاعها، ولعبت النساء دوراً كبيراً في هذه النهضة حتى أوجها في الستينيات، قبل بدء انحسارها.

بعد عقود، صنف أخصائيون في شؤون الجندر مصر في قاع ترتيب ٢٢ دولة عربية في استطلاع للرأي أجرته مؤسسة طومسون رويترز في ٢٠١٣، وأشاروا إلى قوانين تمييزية وتكثّف أعمال العنف والتحرّش وسط تزايد التشدد الإسلامي في أعقاب «الربيع العربي». وفي تقرير صادر في ٢٠١٥ قدّرت وكالة التنمية الفرنسية أن ٣٥٪ من المصريات يعانين من الأمية وعواقبها المعيشية.

أقلّتني رحلتي في سيارة الأجرة المتهوّرة في ضواحي القاهرة، إلى مقر «جمعية نهوض وتنمية المرأة» حيث توفّر حصصاً يومية لمحو الأمية في إطار برنامج من تسعة أشهر مخصص لربات المنزل.

في الحصة الأولى التي حضرتها، أثار وجودي تغامز النساء وضحكاتهن الخافتة. لاحقاً أقرّت لي «أم قمر» أنني ذكّرتهنّ بجاكي تشان، ممثل أفلام الحركة الشهير، فتبادلنا النكات بهذا الشأن في دردشة لطيفة مهّدت للشهر التالي الذي أمضيته بينهن.

ختاماً، طلبت من كلّ من السيدات استخدام مهاراتهن المكتسبة للإجابة على السؤال التالي: لماذا قررتِ تعلّم القراءة والكتابة؟

واستعنت براتبي للتسجل لدراسة العلوم الاجتماعية في الجامعة اللبنانية، بالموازاة مع دروس بالمراسلة في معهد «نيويورك للتصوير الفوتوغرافي».

في ١٩٩٨، غادرتُ الكويت إلى لبنان في سن ٢٢، وبدأت بعد فترة حياتي المهنية في مجال الصحافة، وهو مجال ذكوري بامتياز. لكن بالرغم من انهماكي في عملي اليومي، فإن تجارب نشأتي لم تفارقني، ودفعتني، إلى جانب مشاهدات عملي اليومية إلى البحث عن قصص شبيهة بقصتي.

خلال أبحاثي الأولى لهذا المشروع في ٢٠٠٩، اكتشفت بذهول لدى اطّلاعي على تقرير للأمم المتحدة يعود إلى ٢٠٠٥، أن الدول العربية تسجّل مجتمعة إحدى أعلى نسب أمّية النساء في العالم.

أدركت لاحقا مع تقدّم عملي، أن الأمّية ليست المشكلة الوحيدة امام النساء، بل هناك قيود كثيرة مفروضة عليهنّ، مثل صعوبة الالتحاق بالمدرسة أو معاهد الدراسات العليا أو وقف الدراسة، والبرامج الدراسية الخالية من العلم الفعلي، وضعف الوعي والنشاط السياسي، ونقص الوظائف المناسبة لحاملات الشهادات العليا، ناهيك عن الحروب والنزاعات الداخلية.

هذه العوامل بعض من العقبات الكثيرة التي تشلّ شريحة كبيرة من مجتمعات المنطقة هي شريحة النساء فيها، وتعيق جهود التنمية في جميع بلدانها.

بدأتُ هذا المشروع في ٢٠٠٩، أي قبل انطلاق الأحداث التي سمّيت لاحقاً «الربيع العربي»، واتخذت مسارات شديدة الاختلاف في الدول التي شهدتها.

ففي تونس، حيث انطلقت «ثورة الياسمين» عندما قام شابّ بإحراق نفسه احتجاجا على حياته البائسة، تمكنت البلاد من شق طريقها نحو دستور

تقدّمي جديد، كما أقرّت مؤخراً قانوناً يجرّم العنف ضدّ المرأة. في المقابل في سوريا، تطوّرت التظاهرات التي بدأت سلميّة إلى حرب أهلية متشعّبة تخلّلها تدخل لاعبين إقليميين ودوليين، وما زالت عواقبها تقلب حياة الملايين رأساً على عقب في المنطقة وأبعد منها. بين هذين النقيضين، ما زالت دول كثيرة تواجه تبعات متفاوتة، يشكّل التعليمُ غالباً ضحية أساسية لها.

في الموازاة، أصبح المشروع رحلة تحوّل شخصي ومهنيّ لي، وأثّر على عملي ونظرتي إلى الأمور وما أسعى إليه.

في الصفحات التالية حاولت التقاط لمحات من حياة نساء عربيّات اتّخذن خيارات غير متاحة لهنّ بالعادة في المنطقة، سعياً لتحسين حياتهن وحياة أطفالهن ومجتمعهن.

يشمل المشروع بعضاً من اللقاءات الأكثر تأثيراً عليّ مع شابات أو ربات منزل مخضرمات مذهلات، تمتّعن بالشجاعة ليكنّ رائدات في تطوير المعايير الاجتماعية السائدة في سعيهنّ إلى تعزيز مساهمتهن في عائلاتهن ومجتمعهن.

كما أردت اتخاذ مقاربة تعاونية مع النساء اللواتي صوّرتهنّ، أردت أن يساهمن مباشرة في هذه التجربة بطريقة تنعكس في الصورة النهائية. لذلك أتت كلماتهن المكتوبة بخطّ اليد، لتُكمل الصور وتعبّر بلسانهن عن التزامهن وانجازاتهن... كأنها ختمهن الخاص.

# مُقدّمة

غمرتني سعادة لا توصف عند تخرّجي من الثانوية في ١٩٩٥. أردت مغادرة الكويت حيث وُلدت ونشأت في كنف عائلة فلسطينيّة سعت الى رزقها في المنفى في الإمارة الخليجية الثرية، ومتابعة دراستي في الجامعة، كسائر رفاق صفّي. لكن والدي لم يشاطرني الهدف، بل أراد أن أتسجّل في دروس «سكرتاريا» لأجد وظيفة تكفي مصروفي اليومي، إلى أن يتولى أمري زوج المستقبل.

«لو وُلدت صبيا، لكنت أنفقت على تعليمك»، قال لي أبي. عبارة سمعتها نساء كثيرات في المنطقة العربية في مرحلة ما من حياتهن، وما زلن.

رغم رفضي للمسار الذي ارتآه والدي لي ومضاعفة عزمي على تحصيل شهادة جامعية، أثار اقتراحه فيّ خيبةً كبرى لازمتني فترة طويلة ودفعتني بعد سنوات إلى البحث عن قصص نساء مميّزات في العالم العربي.

أردت تسليط الضوء على العقبات التي واجهتهن في سعيهنّ للعلم وتناول الدور الذي لعبه في حياتهنّ.

بدأت بعائلتي، حيث تتبّعت في حياة والدتي وجدّتي مآيٍ كثيرة ما زالت تهيمن على منطقتنا المضطربة، من القيود الاجتماعية والدينية والتمييز إلى الاضطرابات السياسية والنزاعات المسلحة المقترنة بتدخل خارجي متواصل.

قطعت جدّتي لناحية أمّي دولت دراستها الابتدائية عندما زُوّجت في سن الـ١٣. لدى قيام دولة إسرائيل في ١٩٤٨ اضطرت مع عائلتها أي والديها وأخوتها إلى الهرب إلى المنفى مغادرين ديارهم في حيفا، على ساحل فلسطين الشمالي. بعد فترة قصيرة توفي جدي، فباتت وحدها معيلةً لثلاثة أطفال. هناك أقامت الأرملة الشابة المُعيلة لثلاثة أفواه صغيرة، فتشبّثت بتقاليدها الاجتماعية المحافظة في مجتمع غير مألوف لجأت لإليها وعائلتها إليه، وانكبت على العمل. بالتالي قامت بتعليم الخياطة في مخيم للّاجئين في الضفة الغربية لكسب رزق العائلة، إلى أن سيطرت إسرائيل على هذه المنطقة في حرب ١٩٦٧، ما حرم جدّتي من مورد عيش أساسيّ.

نشأت أمّي في أوضاع مضطربة، فاختارت تعلُّم مهنة عوضاً عن مواصلة الدراسة الثانوية، وتسجّلت في دروس تجميل في مدرسة مهنيّة. ما أن تخرّجت حتى غادرت إلى الكويت للإقامة مع خالها، وهناك عملت في صالون تجميل لمساعدة والدتها ماديّاً.

لاحقاً تزوّجت بوالدي، وهو لاجئ فلسطيني من لبنان قصد الكويت على غرار الكثيرين آنذاك، بحثا عن عمل في البلد الخليجي الثري مع ازدهار الصناعة النفطية في مطلع الستينيات. حتّم عليها زواجها وفقا للتقاليد السائدة أن تترك عملها وتلزم المنزل لتقوم بدورها الزوجي، فتنجب أطفالاً وتعتني بهم.

لم يكن والدي، المعيل الوحيد للعائلة، يعتبر أنّ توفير تعليم لائق لي ولشقيقتيّ يشكّل أولويّة، ولا سيّما مع ضعف مواردنا. ورغم تفهّمي القيود المالية، شعرت بالخيبة لعدم اكتراثه التام لدراستي وعدم تشجيعه لي لمواصلة تحصيلي العلمي، وهو ما كنت أراه الخيار الوحيد لبناء حياة أفضل لنفسي، والخروج من وضعي كلاجئة من غير جنسيّة في ذلك الوقت.

من المؤسف أن النساء في أغلبيّة دول المنطقة لا يحقّ لهنّ إعطاء جنسيتهن لأطفالهن. فإعطاء الجنسيّة حكر على وليّ الأمر وحده، الوالد في غالب الأحيان. وأنا من بين الكثيرين الذين اضطروا إلى التعامل مع تبعات هذا الواقع، فكنت أحمل «وثيقة سفر» لبنانية فحسب، على غرار والدي، من غير أن يحقّ لي الحصول على جنسية والدتي الأردنية.

في الكويت، لم يكن يُسمح للأجانب بشكل عام بالالتحاق بالجامعة الرسمية، ولم يكن هناك جامعات خاصة آنذاك. لذلك بعد التخرج من الثانوية، عملتُ موظفة استقبال في مدرسة أميركية جديدة للفتيات،

## تقديم حنان الشيخ

أتأمّل في الصور التي أخذتها لورا بشناق للفتيات، للشابات وللأمّهات في أكثر من بلدٍ عربي، من مصر وتونس والأردن إلى غزّة فلسطين، والمملكة العربية السعودية واليمن، فأجدني أصفق لهنّ وهنّ يتعلمن القراءة والكتابة ويخمشن في الوقت ذاته التقاليد البالية بأظافرهن بينما يُعبّئن مستنقعات صدورهنّ بأنفاس الحياة.

لقد أرادت لورا بشناق، بصورها الفوتوغرافية هذه، صورةً بعد صورة، أن نسمع ونرى ونشمّ ونتلمس هؤلاء اللواتي نقبن الطرق المسدودة حتى لو كان ذلك بحجم ثقب إبرة الخياطة وانطلقن عبره إلى فضاءات الحرية ولا سيما حرية الاختيار.

نجحت لورا وهي تكمش بعدستها حياتهن، فجاءت كل واحدة من صورها عبارة عن قصة من الواقع. هي احتفاء بالأنثى، بربات البيوت اللواتي أمسكن بالحرف وبالكلمة كأنها طوْق النجاة بعد أن كانت بعيدة عنهن كبعد النجوم عن الأرض. وكي لا يتأخّرن عن اللحاق بقطار الحياة، ينشدْن العلم والتخصص من أجل أن يصبحن أعضاء فعالات في مجتمعاتهن. لكن هذه الصور هي أيضا أشواك في عين المشاهد. فأنا مثلًا لم أستطع إلّا أن أشهق استنكاراً للظلم الذي لحق بالأنثى وأبعدها عن المدارس لمجرّد أنها أنثى. وتأخذنا لورا إلى تلك الشابة على شاطئ البحر بغطاء رأسها الأزرق بلون المدّ والجزر كأنه ما حفلت به حياتها من تقدّم وتراجع.

إلى تلك التي في الخيمة تعزف العود الذي حاولت أكثر من جهة اختطافه من حضنها لأنها أنثى. أرى الشابّة المحجّبة وهي في كامل زينتها كأنها تريد أن تقول، «إني أتحجّب على مزاجي».

وأسمع مَنْ تقول، «لا أريد حارساً بل زوجاً صديقاً»، وأخرى تهتف ضد مقولة «الزواج أو القبر»، وواحدة تتساءل، «هل ستمشي الحياة معي يا تُرى، أم ضدي؟»

الظلام يخيّم في غرفة إحداهن في غزّة جراء انقطاع التيار الكهربائي، فتستعمل هاتفها الخليوي مصدرًا للإضاءة. ويبدو أن بشناق اعتمدت على نور قلوب من التقطت صورهن، وخفقات تلك القلوب بدلاً من اللجوء إلى الأضواء الصناعية، فجاءت صورها بمثابة لوحات فنية كلاسيكية يغلفها الضباب تارةً والنور والظل تارة، فتبدو ألوان الطبيعة أو جدران الغرف كأن الزمن مرّ عليها وغفا أو استيقظ. الأعين في الصور هي التي تتحدث إلينا كأن المصورة قبضت على تعابير النفس بعدستها قبل أن تهرب.

وأنا أصبحت سجينة هذه الصور، أستعيد عبرها حزن أمي كاملة حين كانت تقصّ عليّ ما قالته لعائلتها وهي في الثانية عشرة من عمرها، «أريد أن أذهب إلى المدرسة، حتى الحمام يذهب إلى المدرسة». إذ إنها كانت تراقب كيف كان الحمام يفهم ويتجاوب مع ما كان يطلبه منه «كشّاش الحمام».

بقيت أمي «جاهلة»، تتظاهر بالإغماء وتدّعي المرض وهي على متن الطائرة، كي لا يعرف أحدٌ أنها تجهل القراءة والكتابة ولا تعرف كيف تملأ بطاقات الدخول التي توزع على الركاب.

تعودت على رجاءات أمي، إذ كانت تقول: «لِمَ لا تكتبين قصة حياتي؟ ربما تكون أكثر جمالاً أو سحراً من أي شيء نشرته».

كنت أصم أذني إلى أن قالت ذات يوم: «لم أكن يوماً يائسة لأني لا أقرأ ولا أكتب مثلما أنا الآن، وإذا لم يكن السبب شيئاً آخر، فهو أن أكتب قصة حياتي. دعيني أخبرك كم هو مؤلم أن تهزمك قطعة من الخشب وقطعة من الرصاص.»

وعندما سألتها ماذا تقصد أجابت: «أليس قلم الرصاص مصنوعاً من الخشب والرصاص؟»

أشعر بتقدير عارم تجاه جميع النساء اللواتي فتحن لي قلوبهنّ ومنازلهنّ لأشاطر قصصهنّ. هذا الكتاب لهنّ ولجميع اللواتي تولّين تمهيد السبل للآخرين.

محتوى

| | |
|---|---|
| ٧ | تقديم حنان الشيخ |
| ٨ | مقدمة |
| ١١ | مصر: دروس محو الأمية ٢٠٠٩ |
| ١٥ | الأردن: جليسات المنازل ٢٠١٢ |
| ١٩ | اليمن: الحصول على فرص التعلّم ٢٠١٢ |
| ٢٣ | تونس: اتحاد الطلاب ٢٠١٣ |
| ٢٧ | السعودية: نساء عاملات ٢٠١٦ |
| ٣١ | غزة: الخاتمة ٢٠١٦ |

# I READ I WRITE

أَنَا أَقْرَأُ أَنَا أَكْتُبُ

LAURA BOUSHNAK